The
Ideal
City

The
Ideal
City

ROBERT DICKERSON

Library of Congress Control Number: 2013906130
ISBN: Hardcover   978-1-4836-1930-9
                 Softcover   978-1-4836-1929-3
                 eBook   978-1-4836-1931-6

This book was printed in the United States of America.

Rev. date: 12/18/2013

To order additional copies of this book, contact:
Xlibris LLC
1-888-795-4274
www.Xlibris.com
Orders@Xlibris.com
128604

To Marlin

CONTENTS

The Ideal City

Consider this marvel of Renaissance wit:
The Ideal City, by Lucian Laurana-
See how the canny master contrived in it
To lead the eye along the polished piazza
Back to a single point on the far horizon
By dint of planes, formed by the great arcades
Of noble pallazi, their window-lit facades
Tinted shades of gold and green and dun:
At center fore, a temple, double tiered
Whose coffered, greatly-pedimented doors
Are gained by a shallow flight of marble stairs;
All around, the whole is pillastered
By half-columns crowned by leafy capitals
While over the roof, so gently conical,
Capped with a charming, fluted filial
Is heaven's azure dome, sub-tending all:
The fore-ground, too, is decked with well-wrought wells
Calyced alike with steps octagonal.
No pollution, smog or plastic waste
Mars the sheer perfection of the place
All is open, peaceful, clean and clear
With Harmony and Truth presiding there.

But, world-acquainted traveller, take note
In the houses and street no human can be seen!
Could the great Laurana have forgot
Or did he decline to limn one in?
The palaces, the fountains and the square
Unpeopled, quite, as daydreams sometimes are
Bask in a holy silence still unbroken
By racous laugh or flimsy promise spoken.
No despoiling image of a man!
Painter's irony? Mere poet's spleen?
Or is it, must it, be so them,
That the Ideal City's the city without men?

The Seagull

One day in the hot sun, under a mackerel sky
on a bench in a parking lot, waiting
for a bus to Kingston Station, wielding
fans, we found ourselves approached
by what? a lost-looking seagull—
bow-tie-less, but in charcoal
tails and light gray vest,
waddling formally toward us.
'Now, what,' I wondered, pulling my feet in
and abruptly sitting up, 'could it possibly want with us.
Spare change?' So far from the sea
Did we look like sardines? I watched, as
its webbed toes drily patted
the sun-softened tarmac; as it padded closer
on stalks half-lit like hollyhock stems
I saw in a painting, once.
There was much to admire
in the feathery plush of its breast
whitecap-white but whiter when the breeze blew it back;
I clucked at the way its head swiveled
smoothly, side to side, like a rudder;
chuckled at the way its scimitar beak,
yellowed and notched, swerved
this way and that, like a tiller;
Laughed out loud the way
the alarmingly large bird (two foot)
stopping short of our penumbra, studied us
from out one viridian eye, with hope
and alternately, from the other, with suspicion.
Strange. But still it came.
What did it see in us? We had no wings.
Popcorn, french fries, doritos—the usual enticements—
maybe it was just people-watching.

At any rate, looking it full in the current eye,
I shrugged, brushed myself off, stood stiffly up.
It squealed, wheeled, aimed itself at the shore,
hopped a few steps, lifted its wings
wobbled into the air, planed
off into the grey, over the cars, over roofs
and canopies, green, tan and bone;
over heads of dozing passengers,
bent over their timetables
and disappeared in the shimmer
just as the bus arrived, the sixty-four—
the same beefy lass driving as before,
so we rubbed that bird, too, from our eyes,
gathered up our gear, boarded the bus
fed the fare box two bucks and wondered how
the meeting was important, certain it was.

Reality

As I go walking through the mead
I ask the heavens, high above
How much, at last, of love is *Need*
How much of need is *Love*.

There's a need bereft of love
That isn't what I'm thinking of:
I diss the cash I sorely need
And there's an un-enamored greed.

But is there love prevailing still
Above the house, beyond the will
Where people say 'I think you're great'
And mean not, merely, your estate?

Was there ever, then or now
A perfectly indifferent pal
Who answered you a simple 'wow'
At every triumph, great and small;

Alike ignoring gain, gainsay,
Emotional or any other—
Wasn't Jesus, by the way,
And wasn't, by the way, your mother?

Heaven often answers them
Who imprecate its azure, so,
It moved some clouds to spell 'ahem,
The answer that you seek is 'No'.'

Dedication

When the sea leaves the shore dry
When the seven stars
That fly before Orion
Snap their tethers and elude him,

Leaving him in tears
Then will I leave you, my dear
Till then, we're a pair
And will never sever

Here or in heaven, and I swear
By all things beautiful and rare:
Dews, May's breeze, the choruses from Daphne,
To be yours foreverever.

Whales

I can recall a time
far away and long ago
before my untried eyes had seen an one
the sea was shallow and the sky was low,
and like a word patiently awaiting
its compliment of rhyme
I longed to see them
never knowing when or how
or why they'd cross my bow.

But now the windshield wipers of my mind
can't beat fast enough to clean them
or to make them vanish, and I find
peculiar order in this moving mayhem:
Indigo, above, and dun; below,
and that peculiar color (or non-color),
brighter, now, now duller,
that predators above may see a stone
while those below may see the sky alone.

All so very, very
supernumerary
there and here abounding,
breaching, blowing, sidling, sounding
down to where consciousness is murkiest—
to where the eldest dreams are thought to rest
chins upon the endless toils
of their tails,
there to sleep and unmolested rest.

Single-sole or two by twain or threne
by threne they flail the blue-confronting-blue
which is, finally, the horizon,
with their tremendous tails and gullets of baleen
sad to have grown so small
compared to their immense forbears, and dull—
mindful how the sea's past denizons—
(twice as long and thrice as green)
had skill to sift delusion from the True.

There is a moment before all that follow:
you know what each succeeding one will bring—
What it hasn't yet but will allow
even before its fellows fall a-following
So though your watch has stopped
you know exactly how the hour will on.
I don't know why we know it, but we do—
I call it 'memory-anticipation';
Flat and glassy-blue

the sea shifts and smiles in its sleep and gleams
a-glitterglow with fiery, blinding spangles
bothering the heart with expectation
of where it next will part and issue all at angles
whelk-stuck jaw or ragged flukes or dripping fins
We know they'll appear, the dripping fin
s, that is, but never when. So ocean dreams
its own prodigious themes
and keeps us guessing how and where and when.

While down below there comes, there goes
leviathan; the patient cows
study, pondering, the stubbly hulls
of tide-dividing ships and such-like caravels—
wondering be they friend or foe
that over the waterline
hurtle and torpedo
all so recklessly without a goal,
and shiftingly recoil,

And from their ocean lair
streaking toward the surface scrim,
hurl themselves into the burning, sun-choked air
maybe to free
themselves of barnacles and other feeble vermin
or maybe just to see
whoever their oppressors might so be—
these interlopers on their turf
who drown and disappear and weep and laugh.

Once I saw one caper-toss
and filling all the skies
burst into a thousand birds—
pelicans and terns and plover
and the mighty, shadow-casting albatross,
and uttering myriad cries
flap away, flap away, over
the horizon to the end of day
and disappear to come again no way.

A Steeplechase

I will pass you.
You won't.
I will beat you out
Don't even think of it.
Out of my way, comrade
Bloody bloke.
Mind the breach. Over!
That was a big one.
Onward, onward
I shall win, finally!
Not while I'm here.
I love you in the abstract, but hate you, face to face
Take that!
Ow.
Bloody race. Bloody steeplechase
My life is your death.
Your death is my life.
Disappear!
I won't
Is this necessary?
For the moment.
Is it warm in here? Is it dark?
Don't be silly. It's the hour of 'rush.'

Hasn't it been a while?
Wuss. What about it?
Can't we quit, now?
Never! Those are the rules.
How did I get into this?
Better not ask, if you're a man.
There's a 50% chance I'm not.
Your problem. Outta my way!
Bloody horse race
Without horses, yet
Who shall win the purse? The glorious winner's crown
Who shall disappear in that lake? Drown in ecstasy?
Me. I shall be that drowned fly.
No, me, me
Idiots! Only me.
What's that ahead?
The finish!
How big it is! How it shimmers! It breathes. It seems alive.
Oh, it's alive, believe me.
It beckons! I want to go there.
Fool!
What are those things stuck all over it? Those tenacles?
Dunno. It hardly look Elysian, though.

Not like what you thought.
Not Elysian? Forget it.
Somehow I know that's my goal.
Me, too. But being faster, stronger . . .
Me, too. But being smarter . . .
Me too. But having a beautiful singing voice . . .
Get out of here!
Me, too. My father was a general . . .
Hey, that's against the rules!
We'll see
Yes, we'll see
Here it is! Ready? May the best man win
How confusing. It's huge! Like f-ckin' Oz!
Altogether now. Summon your will! Attack! I mean—swarm!
We have met the enemy . . .
Alot like dragon-bashing, only more bloody fun.
Only not as dangerous.
You think?
Yuck! I'm going home.
Forget it You can't. Ever.
Win or die!
That's the spirit!

Our Love

'Our love will never last a week, I fear—'
That's to say t'will last a hundred year:
As long as mortal flesh can cling to bone
Some part of my affection you will own.
Our persons are of very different sorts—'
That means the Gemini cannot purport
To shine in equal parity as we,
Certain as spectography;
'Our fortunes are of greatly different share—'
That's to say we both, in kind, are poor,
For one man's simple is another's sumptuous fare;
'But I'm a royalist and you're a Tory—'
That's to say that Love will end the story
Of rich, poor, infamy and glory.

Old Photo

Like a land-locked sea, slowly drying up
From the edges in, till only
A splash of its former self—your long dead relations
The island survivors you knew them—
This old photograph, gnawed by the light, fades away.

Here, in pearls, is your lovely mother
In starched collar, your matinee idol father
Here your aunt, before spinsterhood set in
Posing before the prom.
And look at that furniture!

It has something to do with the light.
The fingers of the light rub the borders of the lake
Like Time. And chemistry, that we must also say
Without really knowing why.
Anyway, it all fades—

Inevitably—for hide it,
Hang it in the dark or otherwise
Stopper the light, it still
Slides in like a tide, yawns like a drop-off,
Reaching in a hundred years or so, their knees.

Planxty

'Harpsong
forbidden
strummed in secret or plucked out
at the harper's peril, the strutting tunes, lyric lessons
of musical hedge-schools; needed
treacle of weddings and funerals,'
thought Turlough O'Carolan,
gripping her mane
and bending his back to the back of the mare,
bumpily trotting the bad roads
beside watery green
boglands and sea-lanes and fields of moraine,
and peaks that, clouds dropping coverlets on,
vanished, then glimmered back into view.
Harpsong
rain-patter—
ceaseless as the dew
lodged in the rain
from raindrops born;
to westward—the warmth of sealight:
lured his crumbling vision:
light, viewed through squares of blur—
minimal, miasmal
light even a blind man could see:
sealight; genial and diffuse.

Harpsong—
the poem-preceding tune following after
'Boy,' he shouted, to the darkness ahead, 'boy!'
They were late, but only a day or so.
Late for the feast—but 'what so.'
folks would wait a week,
'Yes, sir?'
for they needed him—in his way
as important as the bride. Needed him,
as people rarely need a blind man—to begin
'so,' he repeated, repeating
snarkily, 'Let them wait.'

The Nightingales of Platres

How they looked I haven't a clue and never will,
so don't ask, I never saw them
though it would seem
they all lived together in a wood atop a hill
for more or less forever,
back to where one traced the liens of their song—
and slept rather drowsily all day long,
wing holstering bill
dreaming the dreams that nightingales daydream;

But by night came clamorously alive, cadenzas
floating across the chasms of dark to the Helvetia's
high-set window.
far above the car park far below
more, itself, than a little ways away
and alot like Juliets', I'd bet; from there you heard them sing—
and spied along the mountainside
moonlit tributaries gleam, winnowing,
the wetlands from the dried.

From there you thought to, if you didn't really see
(Not as if you were a flea
and rode one's neck's downy mottle),
them descend to the watery muddle,
of the stream's edge,
and very much like an hydraulic dredge
ferry mud and other twills
dripping, in the trowels of their bills
while the flood, love-driven, purled and whispered by;

Explode into air and ferry back
homewards to the dark, hill-forests
bills full of mortar to shore up their nests:
Patching up gaps and fissurings
worn there by the weather, where the moon shines through,
And so, so burdened, shuttle to and fro
threshing the night air with their blunt wings—
their masonry, a cause for celebration
though some would claim it merely love's elation

That they whistled, tooted, brayed, invisibly;
mewed, shot songs from the splays of crofts
in wild runs and eerie scales, aloft,
arpeggios trilled and antiphons, quite manically.
Acciaccaturas, every bit as frantically—
whether you heard reclined
head-bent-back-against-the-stead
marveling, half-asleep, wound
in an unwinding sheet, or whether instead

You heard their singing by your high-swept windowsill—
sound drizzling down through your brain's tremendous sky
like the lit trails of fireworks what stain
the starry dome and, in the river, disappearing, die,
they sang the same, but kept invisible
Knowing, perhaps, you'd hear them best, unseen
Or, likelier still, they couldn't care less,
wholly oblivious,
to how you heard their songs, or if you did at all.

So long as their lairs were buff and good
to serve as choirs from which to sing—
scorning birds of lesser skill
who did, after all, what they could and will.
For them, I guess, it was eternal spring
even in December, blear,
which all the world made pleasant
even when it very wasn't,
to the pleasure and vexation of each listening thing.

And I found, from so high up there, that just
as their wings lifted them up into the skies,
(passing through the harp-strings of their song)
a listener got lifted into visions
nothing, mind you, you could trust
or hold for very long:
hookahs amidst carpets stained with flower-colors
saffron heaps and snow-clad peaks and dark-eyed houris,
dervishes a-whirl and dancing janissaries.

Why, thanks to these, I saw the sultan walking with his wives
one night, one than the next more laughing-beautiful
along a cloudy divot, resembling a carpet
in the moon's bright light, so blue and full.
What surprise when on the carpets pile
all began to weave and smile
under a baldachin of gold and silver leaves
only to vanish, never seen again
once they finished their refrain.

Moth To Flame

Moth to flame:
'some other time—
I'm going home,
'thanks all the same.'

Mars The God

Through Narcissi I see stubborn
clouds that wheel and growl
quitting heaven's field.
Water resumes it's weaving.
A wind-torn pool images
a blackly naked branch.

Fawn-dropping time.
Roman January.
Our life begins.

Sorry, sorry, sorry
I am not sorry.

The Plants

One sun becomes them all,
One heaven above.
Feet have all in common soil
Different though they be
So oddly will they show their tolerance and love,
Their eagerness to grow
Tangle, mingle and divide
Bloom, if they can, conditions meet:
So have no fear—
Give them room, the boon of water
Sunshine's glinting glance
And there is little you can do
To stop them, even if you would;
Watch them wind and tilt
And appose their lips
Or lift their leafy wings
From an earth they cannot quit
That about them, stubborn clings,
Good guests, good host
The least to do to make of it the most
And with nonchalance, perchance
Yield a field flower or fruit
For our delight or table fare
Or the hair
Of a lady, needless of the art.
For where they open up their eyes
The skies are blue and clear
The winds are balmy and there lurks no pain
Sharper than the evening rain
May cause, while moths criss-cross the tilled terrain.
There is nothing you can do
That proves your mettle better

Than to take from and give back to them.
If you fail in this
Bitterness will follow bitterness
Poison kiss will follow poison kiss
But if one of these
Prospers from your husbandry
Men will love you and all women miss.

The Woody

Heaven, it's past seven
    time to throw the covers off!
        The sun is shining through the blinds.
          And, well, can you beat that—?

A tremendous woody!
    Sparking a kind
      of festal
        meditation:

Why so full, my son
    of criminal elan,
      half bacchante
        half puritan,

Detected Falstaff
    dancing juego-putto
      Aren't you the happy
        burden of men?

Where do you hope to go, little man?
    Don't smirk—
      you're not the only one
        so what's your plan?

Where you come from don't ask me.
    Heck, if I know—
      these things
        largely beyond control.

Brief,
   and amounting to shadow.
     But well you account
       for that dream, last night

When the wan moon wore
   earrings, pendanted
     with diamonds dangling more
       diamonds in a blue-satin sky;

Nice work, I'd say,
   Woody, (for that's your name).
     You are welcome in my home
       anytime, by the way

However long or short a stay
   'cuz though you wear me out
     I miss you when you're gone
       oh prodigal, my son.

Welcome, welcome,
   wheresoever you come from:
     I admire your drive.
       I'm content when you arrive

For me, you bear no shame.

In the future

In the future, no one will use their birth names
It will give no one agita to coin extra names and personae.
It will be natural to suppress core data,
Such a ruse now useful—essential to survival—
Allegiance to a biological family bogue—even boring.
Here will be the answer to computer compiled records.
All will have closets of identities, distinct as bank accounts.
Industries will generate identities for the sheepish.
Bills will be addressed and paid by dualing identities
The meaning of fake and alternate will become vague ·
Variants of the same person will commit crimes, do good deeds.
Official alternates will marry each other and breed.
IVF via surrogate will become the norm.
Natural history will favor only the flexible.

Bazaar

Man of the world, I pass
the carousels of gold and silver chain,
glittering stones for crushing,
earrings and finger rings,
bracelets and wristlets,
cartons of stuff, satins and silks,
purple-violet carpets, hand-loomed,
rolled and stacked;
chattering budgies, milk-white turtles,
shrieking peafowl, squealing piglets,
dates, figs, currants, prunes,
heaps of spices, saffron and paprika,
jars of incense and frankincense,
pistachios, pecans and almonds.

Wind

'It issues from the tops of trees
born from the gyrations of their limbs;
from there it flies straight to the equator,
circumnavigates the globe, then goes on
to generate the tides . . .'

What? Stop the video. That's ridiculous!
Not scientific really,
but a plausible theory;
when you don't know what's what
take care whose opinion you trust:
Earth, once viewed as flat, is round
and Truth, a powerful sound—
but doubt makes Truth honest

This Morning

This morning
on the train
a mouth so
troublingly wide
and eyes, in a flash,
there and gone;
that looked into mine
like flesh from flesh,
asunder torn, there
and gone.

St. George

Improbably he veers and peers at us—
not the dragon-demon at his feet,
the argent steed, whose sire, Pegasus,
ferried the Perseus
down the wild, airy steep.

and pledges with his sapient, little face
his Rider, the amazing savior,
mail clad form of scarcely bearable grace
trust without measure, endless faithfulness.
So shall we pledge Jesus, Our Redeemer.

But this dragon is not the fish of tufa
that slid barnacle-encrusted
out of the pearl-stuck grotte
to menace golden-haired Andromeda
while the king lamented:

this is the Fiend, the Evil One, the Liar
who prowls the world plotting the soul's ruin
who blisters in Ghehenna-fire.
All that stirs in the night, all that conspires
for chaos, void, ineffable confusion

feels this wound—trembles despairs.
Content, the kings' heart breaks. Perhaps he dies.
The Cross takes root. Exquisitely it bears.
The virgin may continue with her prayers,
rapt, beneath his gently lowered eyes.

Scarecrow

I am a scarecrow.
I watch the clouds
glide across the sky
to and fro
as the winds blow.

Rooks and crows
slide across the sky;
they fear me. Why?
being but paille and chaparral—

my head a bag of straw
Oh, the crows
cry caw-caw
that's the only
song they seem to know.

My hat, a sunflower.
Seeds of the standing Weeds
take their rest
in its nest
and sprout and root and grow.

The Penitant Cat On His Deathbed

I've been a pretty good pet
overall and done what's hoped of me
I've sat on a tuffet with frigging Miss Muffet
all the livelong day
and never run up a tree.

I've kept the panther at bay
that paces in my heart
back and forth and back;
never sprayed or clawed the furniture
but mewed and looked up:

Never bit the vet
or brained a bird
but ate the wretched mix
that probably made me sick,
pretending to like it lots;

Caught an occasional rat,
and, though my pupils swam
like goldfish in a bowl,
never wet the rug:
I simply can't do that.

Plenty of things I never did, ok?
like get involved with bad cats
that sit in the moonlight all night
and raise Cain, Nope. I did not that,
nor swung drunk on a side of beef.

Nosiree on the whole,
in general, nosiree—
I even had a family,
I'm not sad to say
and though I can't recall

just when or how
my little bag of lives got all used up,
it did.
'*C'est la vie*-or, '*c'est le mort*,
as a dog friend once said.

So I've gotten right
with the Big Kitty, and all,
and when I die, as soon I shall,
I'm sure to go straight up, you know,
to that big cat house in the sky.

'Round The Corner

The mouse run 'round the corner
The mouse run 'round the corner
a mouse ran 'round the corner
an' straight up down the hall

Pretty much dun all over
pretty much dun all over
pretty much dun all over
By the light of day she run.

Her putty tail a-flyin
her putty tail aflyin
her putty tail a-flyin
dividin' the hurryscurry air.

She vanish in the floor shine
he vanish in the floor shine
they vanish in the floor shine
and into the puddle sun.

We laugh all day Black Friday
we laugh all day Black Friday
we laugh all day Black Friday
and all the whole day before.

And all the day before, now
and all the day before, now
and all the whole day before, now
at folks that flock to sales.

The mouse run 'round the corner
the mouse run 'round the corner
the mouse ran 'round the corner
and straight up down the hall.

Rainbow

Along a sky of jumbled gray
ominously lit the hues of roses
a rainbow plied its spectral way
clean from Queens to Sheepshead Bay
tempting Wordsworthian apotheoses.

Counting the separate bands
I stopped to study it
measuring its span
carefully on guard against elan
certain it would wane in just a bit.

Hadn't we seen this sort of thing before?
'Casual beauty stalks the town
only to strike and disappear!'
Awe to pay too dear-
nobody likes a letdown.

And there were still a million things to do
Time is money, money time
errands to run and places to go-
Wasn't the mundane the heavier of the two
weighed by the sublime?

'Why', I guess, '*yes*, if we let it';
and summoning oppositional zeal,
dropped the boxes at my feet
choosing the fading marvel in the street
thinking it better, momently, to feel.

Puddle

I am a puddle
picturing the moon
pretty little
pretty shallow
richer by a pebble—
splashed, I recover myself.

Pollywog

Divvying the bog
with its phlegmy flail
the wobbly pollywog
(digesting its tail).
into a muscular frog
gears its porous omnibus;
hauls itself up on hardening limbs
aboard a log with little fuss;
sings all night long
to no appreciable applause;
cocks its spring
jumps, nabs a moth on the wing
and in the midst of splash, slips
back into the syrupy, methane-breathing murk.

Perugino

I am the greatest painter who ever breathed.
Any fool enough to dispute this claim
Should simply inspect my work in the Cambio
At Perusia, in the college of that name.
Or better, see my Ascension, which so pleased
the hosts, et al, at cleanly San Pietro.
Sure there's good work done in Florence, too-
Up there everything's Leonardo, Leonardo!
A few in Flanders know a thing or two
But no one, no one, beats the Perugino,
Present or past, in these Italian hills
So help me God. But yesterday, I swear,
I saw an angel by my young student Rafaels'
So fine—my God, I fear you love him more!

Non-Rose

Non-roses, yellow frills of knitted dew,
airy apparitions
flapping your stiffening robes like houris, dancing veils,
along the jagged branches of a non-bush—
I pluck you not.

And why not not?
There's lots not to pluck.
The blank book of life that shuts with a bang so full
of endless. dizzying doings,
stays obstinately closed.

By your hand shield your eyes.
Don't stare. Ignore.
Bothersome muses of the void
before the collect

never let your gaze
graze or take print
of this Veronica veil, the morning,
and to God
whose gifts aren't worth it,
wheelbarrow them back.

Nature

Nature cruelly tricked the human heart
with splendid feathers, well-designed for flight
but feet denied it by capricious Art
assuring that it never might alight
or rest content within its chosen croft
but always must shriek forth its fierce lament
weep and circle ceaselessly aloft
and scour the earth for haven without end.
Sometimes on the false limb of the wind
it rests and breathes a brief respite:
so for one consoling spark of light
their shrunken eyes are battered by the blind:
then the wind folds it soldiers on.
the spark dies and all is dark again.

Marilee

If I could capture
the sheen on your shoulder
in my bare hands,
Marilee, Marilee,
brighter than moonshine
I would take it home
to fly around the room
live there and die there
by its inspired light
sleep by day and read away
the long winter's night.

Mule

Smarter than a horse
Hardier than an ass
Laughing exclusion to the rule
Unbroken to bridle, saddle
Mover, shaker, acre-breaker
Eager to work, loving the course
Minding not the goal
Loathe to foal
Ladies and gentlemen
Here is the mule: the
World looks different
Through his ears.

A True Story

(To Dr. Larry Smith)

At a quarter past the hour there came a knock at the door-
it was Giorgio, late as usual.
'Giorgio. you're late', I yelled from my seat.
I knew it was him. He had a very personal knock
Besides, I was expecting him.

It was getting dark. That's not true-it was dark already
Traffic on the Avenue was jammed. Horns were wailing
Head lights, street lights, on,on.
What excuse would he give this time?
Giorgio was what we called a 'space cadet',
from what you might call 'generation text',
as many my age would agree
Brooklyn born, his name despite,
Giorgio was likeable, if distractible.
but I was not prepared for what came next

'Doc. there was this fascinating show on TV-
I mean FAS-cinating. I couldn't stop watching.'

'Oh', I said, without much interest,
irked to be undone by a re-run.

'It was called 'Grimm's Stories'. On channel 31
There's lots. Have you heard of them?

'Uh-huh', I replied, looking at my notes,
'I've heard of the Grimm's things-
somewhere along the line.'

'Well this one was about a little guy with a long beard—
him and this chick made a deal.

He'd do all her work for free
if she could guess his name
And she did!'

'Sure,' I said, sitting back,
'I remember that one
It's called . . .'

'So one night she was coming home from a party', interrupted
Giorgio,
'but she had to go through a big forest or something.
Up ahead she saw a bonfire burning—
There was the little man, dancing around the flames!
pretty weird, huh?'

'I've heard worse And then . . . ?'

'Dancing and singing his name . . .'

'So she learned his name?'

'Yep, And, boy, was he mad!
He had to do all her work without getting paid
It was like getting married.'

'Do you remember his name?' I asked,

'Of course.'

'What was it?'

'It was . . . Rumpleforeskin.'

'It was what?' I said, pulling a face. 'Are you sure?'

'Sure I'm sure. It was Rumpleforeskin.'

I sat up, loathe to laugh
'That's not what I remember, Giorgio.
You mean RumpleSTILZKIN-
his name was RumpleSTILZKIN'

'Whatever,' conceded Giorgio. 'Hey, no, it was Rumpleforeskin!
'Why should I say Rumplestilzkin when his name was
Rumpleforeskin?
Trust me on this one, doc'.

'What channel was this?'

'31'

I made a mental note

'And what was his name, again?'

Again, Giorgio repeated his version of the little man's name.

'And, that's why you were late?'

'Uh-huh. Sorry'.

Giorgio was worse than apologetic. He was sincere.
'Rumpleforeskin, Rumpleforeskin', I chanted, sitting back-
it had a certain ring.
Anyway, there was no convincing Giorgio.

'So, Giorgio, how was your week?'

'Let me tell you about it.'

Gulped

Gulped from the hand by the mouth
engulfed by the gut
spilled to the blood
the heart clenched its fist, while the brain
lit up like a fishing village.

Tinos

First, two roosters vying in the dark
cracked the fragile stillness of the night
then the sparrows deafening demot
spread the rift until a golden light
in rivulets fell and filled the window box
putting weak and timid dreams to rout
then the tuneful axle of a cart
kikiriki-drove the darkness out.
A screen door slammed, a first boat quit the sand
a donkey bawled, a whirling swallow swarm
fifed a fray in heaven's sounding bell
Night ran off, his sandals in his hand
Hebe turned into my waking arm
But that is all of Tinos I can tell.

Show Tune #3

What a lovely matinee
intermission was too short
but it's snowing, now, the wind is blowing
do you get my drift,
Baby, can I give you a lift?

Your way and my way
go the same highway
The cabbie knows a byway.
I don't so do say
Baby, I can give you a lift.

In the cab we'll gab,
laugh and count the ways
that life is like a Broadway play
I will only pay if,
Baby, I can give you a lift.

When you get home, bone-dry
you will invite me in
if you've a shred of decency
for a quick one, if,
Baby, I can give you a lift.

I'll say 'no, I gotta run-
Oh, ok, you win.
but, darling, have you any change'?
'I dunno, I'll look.
And, thanks so much for the lift'.

refrain

Toss away that umbrella
you don't need it anymore
just hop inside
Make me a happy fella!
funny how the weather
makes for a pleasant ride
Hurry, the meter's running
Time is money, ah,
it isn't even funny
it isn't even funny.

Seige

'I can't believe it,' murmured old Valette, in toney Italian. 'The nerve!'
His secretary's quip was earthier. He revered the old man and his crazy bravery.
'Who does she think she is? Thanks for nothing. Can she think of no one's interest but her own? A chip off the old block'.
And so on . . .
'Oliver, she's your sovereign.'
Oliver said nothing. True, he didn't like siding against his queen.
'Say naught, regret naught'. But he wanted his loyalties clear.

Looking out the corbelled window, across the harbor toward the ruins of St Elmo's, old Valette watched the crumbled western rampart and the stone-filled moat and the searching figures of the engineers on top. Like ants. He remembered the battle—those long, awful, bloody summer hours and days he would rather forget, but couldn't.
He thought of the men—how bravely they fought, how gladly and horribly they died. Looking nearer, he saw the ochre fronts of cliff-borne palaces. Like graceful out croppings of the limestone they rose from. Both turned fiery gold in the low sun. The in-between stretch of dozing water seemed a pool for descending angels to bathe
in. It turned back the sun's rays. Magnificent.

'As it always would be,' he thought. Thanks to him.
Anachronism, indeed.

But he didn't really say that last part. He just felt it.

Turning from the window and limping to the fireplace, he
swore an expletive in Italian that must have sounded mild to
Oliver's ears.
Without doubt, English was the language of expletives.

On the great, marquinia table, inlaid pink and orange, he
tossed the mockery bearing the English queen's seal with its
manifold stamps and fancy ribbons.
'Thanks. Thanks, thanks. Much indebted . . . Thanks
for . . . thanks . . . thanks, thanks . . . etc.'
-Of course. Don't mention it.
The envoys, who delivered the parchment but couldn't read,
were feasting on plaice and drinking Sicilian wine in the hall,
below.
But the sea was bristling with ships, sailing placidly to Genoa,
Marseilles, and faraway Valencia, bearing wheat and spices
from the Levant and slaves to London.

'Good riddance. And the vile language! Barbaric.

There was lots to do. Old horrors fade before fresh triumphs.
Across the harbor the new city was rising fast. He, himself,
had laid the first stone. Would he live to see it done?
He doubted it. Not the way he felt. But, God willing, he would.
On the mantel the clock chimed six. Along the peninsula, in
each little belfrey, swung a bell on its rung. Soon there were
many, a chorus. They rang a whole minute, then ceased.
Old Valette liked the sound of the bells. He would have a little
dinner, then go to bed.
'And, Oliver—'
'Yes, sir?'
'Go to bed.'

Seven Basic Machines

'First the pulley. With this window washers haul
themselves up to the tip-top or drop'.
'Yes', she said, with minimal interest. 'Next'.

'Then there's the lever. Useful for prising treasure'.
'Very well, she said,' but I can't tell you how I try
never to pry'.

'Well, there's the wheel. Often invented, excellent for gliding
singly, in tandem, in trio or more'.
'Of course', said she, 'and number four'?

'Um', I said, starting to perspire,
and giving my brains a wrench—'the plane, if you desire'.
'I've never been inclined. Continue please'.

'The wedge', I said, recalling that
a wedge could not be beaten for
dividing night from day and dog from cat.

'Then, there's the screw', I muttered, turning blue.
'Let's come back to that.
'Continue'.

'Lever, ah, pulley, plane, wedge, ah, screw, wheel,
What's last'? She thought and thought
and finally calmly cried: 'the high heel'!

Secrets

A secret burns in my brain
like a glowing coal.
A secret, lodged behind my eyes
sputters and mutters like a burning coal
through the long lights of York
singeing its tissuey bed
burning its keeper.

How it longs to slip the keep of its living brazier
To give itself to the world at least in part
perhaps to, credence given, start a small fire-

How it yearns to hatch out
like a chick from an egg
and trot about the world crying 'peep, peep, peep.'

I, too, crave the secret's liberation
(for it fidgets in there like a bean)
I, too, crave its escape
into the ears of a few.

So would you. It hurts. It's hot.
Its lonely existence serving no purpose
but secrecy, a pretty dull thing,
pointless to all who might wish to hear-

useless to all who might otherwise be listening,
on the phone, propped on pillows, sipping myrthe,
to the enchanting music of the secret, the
serpentine strain, oboed forth,
crossing itself, doubling back.

And this secret is a humdinger.
This secret is an anaconda. It is the Great American Secret.
All other secrets beside it would seem trifles—
Would be shamed back into their coops;
A most delicate secret, this,
concerning as it does a certain person from the Bourse
(a junior vice-president for the firm of Valentino
who is generally acknowledged a non-pareil)
a friend of our dear friend Larry
A secret of treble import and viral ongoingness,
guarded still but for the solvent of strong drink
and told to me by Carlo—his be the shame.
This secret bothers me now—
barks, bays, rattles its chain
paces, ticks the bars with its tin, makes itself a nuisance,
wants out,
insists itself innocent.
Can the secret be blamelessly outed
in the eyes of say, Truth?

I recall now once having read
in I forget which codex anticus
the strict conditions,
rites obscure and rubric byzantine,
that exonerate a teller
forced to disclose a secret:
the conditions arcane,
pertaining to the telling of all secrets,
which essentially all
boil down to three types
according to their species.

First, secrets of *state*, said my codex,
classic examples of which would be the Ems letter
and (doubtless) Irangate.
These may be blamelessly told
after the lapse of three moons.
Whereupon the *Deesse* of secrecy, her complexion avocado,
her temples plaited with slender snakes,
awakens, pardons the indiscretion, then resumes her trance—
during which she listens, vengefully, the wide world over
for the seismic disclosure of secrets
for forgiveness of which, one must burn the stamens of gentian.

Second: secrets of (and this is hard to translate)
secrets of estate—water fountain secrets-for lack of a better term
secrets which pertain to people in the flow of it all
affected by woes
never earned per se
what might be an example?
that so and so is getting a yellow slip,
that so and so is up to her ears in debt,
that someone is not well:
these must be saved for half a year
under pain of the most abysmal Karma
and leaked to no more than two informees
themselves bid to secrecy for a similar time
the better to slow the secret's path through a curious world
the better to calm the snakes.
Telling these secrets, one must burn the pale berries of
mistletoe
Don't ask me why, I didn't make the rules,
I'm just repeating what I read.

But the third kind of secret
is the *heart* secret—
Secrets of things that happen in the dark
between two or more individuals;
secrets which whisper of the wigglings of limbs
and cinematically depict the fissuring and collapse of the will
like a sand-dune sacked by a sirocco.
These are secrets most beloved of the Deesse:
virginal, inviolable,
and while they are young

worthy to be held in utmost confidence
by any man who changes his socks daily,
who has a bank account
or hopes to see his children prosper.
Secrets whose telling may rend
the fragile liens of newly-weds;
interfere where troth is pledged;
that in their very unleashing
start household wars; burn down houses
In which lives and livelihoods are merged,
and costly, new dining room chairs from Henredon.
These secrets must be kept a full half-year
following the telling.
Speak them not!
the risk is huge!
the Furies never sleep-
Sliding her black rainbow,
and pedaling her ball, comes the Deesse-
the snakes awaken
hoods erect,
scowling, howling.

So the secret that currently burns in my brain-
I shall keep fast,
telling not even Jane,
that bat-eared, tympanum of secrets
who is on perfectly good terms with the parties involved.
After all, I, too, change my socks daily;
for the sake of my investments, I shall not;
for the sake of my unborn children, I shall not;
for fear of the Deese, I shall not;
as the chain of red lights ahead blinks green
and the bus jerks into gear, I
shall *not*.

Song/1987

Come back to New York, honeybaby
Give that job a shove
There's so much we can do here-
We can go shopping and
Hettie will cancel my appointments
We can take Friday free-
Anything, anything
To hear your sweet voice again.

Come back to this town honeybaby
Anything you please
Is ok by me: Shea,
The Museum of Natural History
And when it's daytime in Tahiti
We'll go dancing at the Roxy—
Anything, anything
To see your sweet face again.

Take the first plane out, honeydarling
Quit that barbarous shore
Tailwinds favorably disposing
You can be here in three hours;
And you will see the city lights
All sprawled out from the air
Anything, anything
To have you here again.

No one will know, believe me.
I'll not tell a soul.
We'll spend the weekend on the Island
There in the sand I'll scrawl
My name in oil
Along your lovely vertebrae.
Anything, anything, anyanything
To have you close again.

Paul in Tarsus

Much was dear, much unclear.
Clearly he was safer here
where even now his heart would skip
with every unexpected rip
of tent-cloth behind him, after one whole year.

Where even the dark above his head
seemed a creaking cover lid
of woven rushes, through the night
lowering him to safety, and to flight,
flight, flight, as he lay awake in the comfortable bed.

So then why, beside the musical fountains
amidst the placid mountains
of this rather attractive provincial town
that could soften any frown
with gifts of pomegranates, oranges and plantains,

as he sat in the dusky square,
did Peace increasingly appear,
though lovely, composed of fluttering moths,
that breathed into his ear 'I am your Death'?
oh, endless nervousness and hurryings through dinner.

Somewhere a bird was singing loud
as if to waken the errant world
crying 'Saul, Saul, Saul!'
The tide in his eye went dead as a sea-
he saw voyages ahead. Storms. Sweat and blood.

Aria

Bolt upright, plying his lanky frame
and fled by panicky fishes and frogs
Death poles his coffin boat by night
along the shores of an immense lake;
staring at the stars, even Death
is impressed by their numbers

along the shores of an immense lake
the water is black, fretted
with little waves and pointed
with faint light. Drowsy reeds whisper-
scrape along the gunwales, the
up-churned muck has the warm, sweet smell

of an immense lake and Death is singing
an aria about Death
singing an aria by night
in a shallow boat, on a Patagonian lake.
'So many stars', sings Death in the song,
'So many stars'.

Barrio

Today is St. Patrick's Day-but here in the Barrio
there's little green to see
Green is the color of money
there's precious little of that here,
this being the land of Section-8 housing, children
and large, dull-looking dogs with such powerful jaws
one simply moves to the other side of the street
Nevertheless there's color:
there's the red and blue of the triangular flag;
there's the silver moon of the trashcan lid
and the gold of the real moon;
there's the azure pulse of the congas;
there's the yellow of the yellow cabs
speeding down the avenue to the next light;
there's the black velvet of the night sky;
there's the glint of Mars so pink;
and, a sort of electrical ADD—
a share of frantically blinking, left-over Christmas lights
But green-no. you have to go downtown for that-
amidst smiling youth, arms linked
There you'll see green aplenty: seas of it
on the subway, on the buses.
You'll see it on the 3.
A sweater here, a stocking there, a scarf, a tam,
the furtive lining of a necktie.
But here in the Barrio don't look for it-
nor for that famous parade:
green is too much like money
there's precious little of that, here.

Beside The 1925 Hydrant

Beside the 1925 fire hydrant
at the comer of Greenwich and 12th, I—
the sun from the southeast
already so warm it could heat bathwater.
A motor scooter putters by.

On the scaffold of a fire escape, way up,
men, specks of red and blue check,
carefully point the brick without haste
Trees of the old but alert houses
heel into their shutters.
On the doorstep a cat is already asleep.

A.M. Inspection

Some standing tall like officers
Some tumbling down like Jacks and Jills
I pass the troops of daffodils
The Kitchener of the flower wars,

And peer in each canary face
The hope and darling of its race,
Pause to fix a ruff or there
A tuft of cellophane repair.

Grave my soul and full of grief
To see them fluttering stalk and leaf
So fair they are, and I know well
That earth is brief and war is hell.

Nor does it help to hear them speak:
How for the Nation *it is meet*
To perish—all in perfect Greek.
The bitter quarrels with the sweet.

I salute them, one by one
'Remember duty' sternly bid
As off they file en parade
To cast themselves upon the sun.

A Bus Poem

The subway is so foul somedays there is nothing to do
but take off your head and stow it in your bag
as I myself did this morning, boarding the L
A technique learned from my friend Biff the bouncer,
and taking only a little practice to perfect:
the right hand planting a sharp rap aside the mandible
while the left draws the head up smartly by the topknot.

Head in the sack, held securely in the lap
one is spared the slings and arrows of the madding crowd;
the richly stained floorboard; the boogeyman scrawl
effacing the key; a brace of strollers;
humorless faces fluoresced a mortal green
kneading mounds of gum; riveted walls
akin to the color of chicken-skin.

Catcheted thus, much use can be made
of Time lost in profitless nursing of spleen-
Time to brush up on those German verbs;
recall the twelve causes of hypokalemia;
audit the collected organ works of Brahms;
Time to rethink the nicer implications
of the Henderson-Hasselbach equation;

or just lay your head on the socks and relax
quietly dozing, jarred to repose
by the oddly restful song of the tracks-

'hernias need not be a problem'
'if adolescent problems are driving you to the brink'
'squeeze you way to shapely hips and thighs'
'deep asleep, in your beautiful, clear skin'

Faintly then sounds the porter's cry
that normally pierces the ear like an awl
now like a shepherd calling his flock
or conscience's underwater bawl.
Watch out, though. Don't miss your stop
(as I did once, bypassing Wall
waking up, aghast, in Borough Hall.)

Getting where you've gone, simply do as you did
at the outset, only exactly in reverse.
from the dark of the duffle, draw your happy head,
replace it on your shoulders rested and refreshed
sure by the click to be back in thread-
tighten and go forward, suited to face
that miserable boss, that really tough case.

Buying the Prison

The time is now. You have the cash in hand.
Phlox and pansies prink the prison yard
Those who guarded you betimes, you guard
And there is wine enough to soak the sand.
Loves that filled the corners of the cell
Like whirling ghosts, pardoned or escaped
Dash for the sea-shore and pell-mell
Leave you gasping, sighing, ruined and raped
A pretty house albeit square and poor
These four bare walls will make, this rotting floor
The fire flares the way it did before:
The keep, too, you have in peaceful keeping
Enough of gnashing, now, enough of weeping
let there be laughter after easy sleeping

Leopard

A leopard doesn't know he's a leopard-
all that's in your head
frozen by your horror
he'd rather be dead
than monkey with you at all. He
rises from his bed
at red nightfall
when the moon gets extra-big
and the trees get tall,
puts on his spots
draws the dark's long veil
over his head
and bounds away
twirling his tail
elegantly eliding
into the swale;
and slithering up the croft
of a tamarind tree
beside a moon-drenched pond
hangs
dreaming of that delicious gazelle
All so very,
very cool.
And it isn't his fault,
it's not his sin
if you see a man
in leopard skin.

Owl Children

Imagine a roomful of owls—
the little white hopping kind
that hail from the earthen bowers
of the prairie dog tunnels they find,
each chimney capped with a stone.
disdaining the neighboring mice,
that live on seeds alone
and beans, of course, and rice;
You'll need a trowel to retrieve them
and a sack to stow them in.

Oh, that would be so nice-
snowy white owlets everywhere:
owlets on the mantelpiece
and backs of every chair.
They wouldn't defecate or make
an extra work for you.
but minding their business, eightish wake
already asking 'who'?
with feathery bars and stripes and eyes
that silently holler 'boo'!

Owls that slide on the tile
cool their wings at the fan
muster and defile
then fall in league to a man;
double their ranks in the mirror
worry the plants and then
seeing nothng dearer,
nibble the porcelain;
but not before saying 'please'.
and *'gesundheit'* if you sneeze.

All night when you'd be reading
they'd hop about your feet
then comes their leader, leading
more and more in suite;
Up your leg they'd clamber
turn upon your knees
ask who you be reading
whose plume you undertake
and what about that feeding
you promised them to make.

Whether the dead are better off than
we the living, we who
live must ask the dead
who bear the standard of comparison.
Someone once said
'Not to be born is best'.
But living seems better than dying-
that we can say is true,
and flapping about and building nests
is good for people, too.

It Is Better . . .

It is better to make way than to take way
say the soft clouds, they say,
'it is better to rake hay than to make hay-
Come away my way;
Birds, another and another follow
in a wide-careering flight
until the sky's alive with each last swallow
greeting and welcoming the night,
for they can't sleep until they pass this rite;
Spring follows Winter, Summer, Fall-
The sky is wide—by God, there's room for all
Still they cry out loud and still they call
over the sun-struck, undulating bay:
'deniz, deniz', blow pretty breeze',

Like A Hurricane

Like a hurricane
Memory lashes my heart
ravaging coastlands
suddenly veering inland
ushering in floods
silencing its people.

Homes tiddle away
Trees-yanked up like turnips
Goodly crops flattened.
Cars blown over and over,
fender over bumper.
Damage in the millions.

And the bitterness of regret
bubbles up from the heart's core
filling the fissures,
over-spilling sulci
drowning the yellow corn,
drowning the noble wheat.

Lament

the snow falls on my father's bed
on the foot
on the head
the snow falls on my father's bed
all the night and morning long

my fathers' bed is in the ground
his sleep is deep
his sleep is sound
my fathers' bed is in the ground
he will not soon awaken

his earthly day was not so long
but thirty year
or very near
his earthly day was not so long—
the reason more to mourn him

the devil took him by the hand
and turned him on
to heroin
the devil took him by the hand
and that is why he's gone

softly on the dreaming land
sifts and blows
the gleaming snow
softly on the weeping land
and on my father's stone

the snow falls on my father's bed
on the foot
on the head
the snow falls on my father's bed
all the night and morning long.

Jenny Bluet

His mother was Southern
Jenny was her name. Jenny Bluet.
She had the bloodlines, the gold
acres of scratchy tobacco—
The ground where she played was radiant;
His papi tumbled in from Charleston.
She grew to love him
He, too, had a name,
a seedbox and a spaceheater.
They called him Harley
Harvey Trefoil-Bluet-
altogether, so cool.

Capitals

you have taken a dilapidated train to a leaky boat
which ferries you, slowly, to a third world airport
where palm trees struggle against hostile winds
where you board a plane stuck with propellers
that squats at a froggy angle to the tarmac

and muttering *vita brevis est* buckle yourself in,
noticing neither pilot nor stewardess; watch
semiphore the ground crew through a dirty window;
and after an eighteen hour flight, through rain
over turbulent seas, cross yourself,

dive to a landing, disembark, and on foot
trudge on for days, neither eating nor drinking,
until, in their Pleistocene forest you reach them-
slithering, hissing and getting in each other's way;
this is what you've come for. everyone said *No*

They do not exist; yes, they belong to the long ago.
Having no time to exult, you snatch a cell-phone camera
from your jacket pocket and begin to shoot
what you know will make your fortune back home
if you can ever go there, again:—

the gracility of the A—angles and corners despite;
its cross-bar demanding a time-wasting pencil lift,
useful once, now doomed to orthographic limbo; the
fustiness of the B—its double loops
a Darwinian marvel, serving no apparent need;

the C just an impossibly large version of its low-case self
munching its own weight of leaves per day—
shy, up to its belly in a small lake of ambivalence—
a tuber of some sort sliding down its throat,
the D a wind-filled spinaker from the days of sail;

they don't seem dangerous at all.
gradually you lose your fear and begin
to understand why, of doubtful use, they failed to survive
and why their habitat shrank to this far-flung fold-
the revelation strikes you like lightening.

you will show your kid the pictures when you get home.
'yes', you will say, 'that's the way it was—', he will
glance at them, smile politely, make a tactful show of interest
then go back to his business, e-mailing someone in China.
or googling something, capitals not needed, *'natch.*

Erotification

Not rough like a train wreck or a car wreck
or loud like a cat fight or two neighbors
shouting angrily across an alley by night
about nothing much at all; but quietly, more

like rain perturbs the leaves, or snow falls,
or calcium hardens a bone
changing like a diamond squeezed from a coal
over eons, invisibly, underground,

do you proceed, gentle Erotification,
subtly filling the cells of the father, the motherlove—
that elder deemed by the canny child
a better bet for trust and emulation

until the sea changed,
the chord, newly augmented, rings brightly out,
until the tree, dusted with dazzling snow, becomes
overnight the flower of a hitherto secret season

which will endure
giving (or not) it's denizon the Will
to be, in turn, a model for wise children to
worship and eroticize.

A realistic love poem from middle age

I gave my new love flowers-
sleek adolescence
of tulips from California
purple-virginal
cold, too, and dewy
pink and sky green-
hues that will often tint
the lintels of dreams

I wanted to give a gift-
something that would fire,
flare, swoon with chagrin and fade
slowly, beautiful like our
preposterous love: dry up, their dyes
caked in their veins, intact
therefore—flowers opening their beaks
irresistibly to the sun.

Our hourglass, these
tulips in their tall
clear, cylinder of sunshine
confused at the waterline
'Set, go', we cried as one
by one the petals plash
in the warm mahogany sea, their
prows imaged in the polished wood.

When the last petal dropped
and spotted molds in the fell water
gummed the stems, out we flung them
now but fodder for regret;
tenderly, I collected my neckties
from the dear hand, our lips
brushed and we beat it to the corners
of our real-life lives, plaisant, civilized.

Anzio

Sad port of Anzio
you sadden me
Gardens and flowers
bathed in brindisi
melancholy

Fragola cloud
dissolving around
grotto and villa
stone feeding billow
lapping stone

Sad, strange elegy
of wind and sea-spray
entangled by
gone laughter and
the lovers' cry

Drowsy rose
abed in salt air
far too heavy for
your stem to bear
with dewy tear

And you sad, scintillating
scythe of moon,
you ship adrift,
bewitched, without a port
without a home

wound and bless
with homesickness:
chill like a breath
from the vast abyss
my heavy heart

Sad port of Anzio
to my soul you send
resistless restlessness
and such imperfect peace
that at end

I am like a man
in an alien tomb
buried beyond repair
in a foreign land
in a soil not his own.

Bus Poem #8; Penelope

It seems like Penelope's weaving, West 14th Street-
eternally under construction, that is,
yet all gains rapidly unraveled
by night when only the drunks and the tv people
walk the glittering sidewalks, rambling, lost
in their thoughts, talking out their heads.

All summer long, like Penelope's nightly weaving
the ditch undigs itself, the concrete flows
backwards up ghostly troughs
dropped from a thick and wholly starless sky:
the freshly laid asphalt sublimes,
the street unbastes itself along carefully laid seams,
its fresh white line
wound up in a ball
while Penelope herself sits bare-headed
on her bed over Reddens' Funeral Home
weeping into the heat

Each morning the workmen return
like unhidden suitors, loathed but borne,
a keener one occasionally pushing back his hat,
muttering a *parbleu* of dismay, daring not
to be sharing suspicians with duller chums

After all, a job is a job, and one
job being like another, all
jobs are equally ok, and this
is a job.

Dafni

tea of blue smoke, tobac, a
clean-boned man, the
wave, its guilty slope seaward
the jerky fiddlebow and a palm
leaf deftly beguiled-

blow, blow little wind

-quae Cnidon
fulgentesque Cyclades et Paphon.

little wind, little wind

combed sand of burning sign
reedy alphabet, old crows
garment, tasseled for battle camel-
trodden seaward,
Diva!

listen, the wind

Slowly, this morning, one
sees it again
ruddy Barbarossa
missing bottom
gasping Saleph water, the blue
un-beginning, never
ending . . . .

wind, *animateur*, blow
little wind

Chelsea Ramble

I like them, these days
coming from the train
mornings of cool exhalations
summer mostly gone
the sun a broken comb of tawny honey
basting the leaves
of the prehistoric trees
Ginko biloba
fringey maiden's hair
(cures Alzheimer's?)
bluesilver babes
leaning in doorways
thinking of their newboyfriends
thinking of the weekend
or nothing at all but the
flags lifted evenly by the breeze
yellow, rose red, cream of green
imported from Mexico's
imported from Guam's
at truckstop and bus stop
sedums and geraniums
hooped in half barrels
factories, phylacteries,
goods and services
guns and butter;
hammers bang
hoses hose
doorways yawn
gears groan
sparks shoot, saws
circularly whinny
wobbly sheets of clean-pressed metal
shimmer their thunder

flung in stacks
or pressed into artifacts-
collars and elbows
duct-made frames
flex conductors
Cupulae et plena
Brooms brushing tides of filthy sludge
wetly whisper: pho . . .
photo . . . photoshoot
Cafehaberdasherynewdeli
Does it matter, do you know
Atlantic Scaffold
2 Woodland Avenue
Masbeth, N.Y.
your permit has expired?

Congratulations Minuet

congratulations, congratulations con
gratulations, congrats . . .

in a sort of loopy minuet
we fall together, fall apart
then fall together, again

congratulations, congratulations, con
gratulations, congrats.

Florent

Florent, Florent,
that it should pass,
your manic grin,
alas, alas
Florent, Florent
then so now—now so then
Florent, Florent
to a boy from Astoria a
pretty good restaurant:
Florent—
sic transit Gloria

Pinata

Elder

Child. put down that stick-
leave it alone, that piñata
of plied crepe and beads.
Look how it swings so gently on the breeze
knotted to that fork in the tree:
if you fixed a candle in it
it might double as a Chinese lantern—
let's just sit here and watch it swing
pasted on the air before the lake
back-grounded by that mountain peak and star.

Younger

No, it's my birthday
and the piñata is all mine.
It makes me tired to see
how the wind lifts and drops it;
frankly it makes me tired to see it
rock back and forth
like a clapperless bell,
like a metronome-
whose sing-song tyranny I refuse
and I know one thing-
the piñata is full of good things
(pinatas always are)
that spill out to brave boys
who can give them a whack
fissuring papery tissues
spilling out caramels
in golden foils. Mints
light chocolate and dark chocolate,
oozing creams and jellies.
boats with red sails; silver whistles

Booklets and tiddlies
set to leap one another over:
divers that dive and rockets that glare-
No, Uncle, I'm not satisfied with the outside.
no matter how nice I want what's within.

Elder

Child, you have made a choice:
Informed and entirely your own.
Frankly, I prefer my chair
my easel and my guitar:
Frankly, I'd rather watch the breezy
undulations of what doubtless is
the centerpiece of the feast.
Just remember: you can't take it back—
Once the piñata is torn
it can never be turned
into a lantern or any beautiful thing
(not that it isn't beautiful enough, spilled.
You can't collect the fallen sweets and toys
once in the dust.
Watch or play—these seem to be the choices,
both have merit
Would it were otherwise,
but it's not.
So here, take this stick-
(I'm giving you mine)
It's your birthday-the pinata's yours:
Give it a whack
and bring me candy, too,
or a sailing ship,
hurry, but just one.

Interlude

Halfway 'round the world and more
huffing and puffing, I have come
and stretched myself along this pier
to slumber in the morning sun.

The waters purl and slap and hiss
beneath my head, while in the depths
little fish hang motionless.
A sunbeam penetrates my breast

Where did I see it all before
but in a dream? the little town,
the Virgin-guarded harbor where
the painted boats bob up and down.

We longed for it, this motionless
deep slumber in the morning sun-
know it when you find it, Peace,
it was for this that you had come.

Lot

'Don't look back—
need I remind
you'?, warned
the angel, ahead.
'Ok', said Lot—
'I'm trying. I'm trying
to do what you said—'
while the town behind him burned;

But he wanted to be sure
his daughters complied:
one covered her face with her veil;
the other tied
a sash around her eyes
and limped along;
only his salty wife
dallied and turned.

'You need't remind me',
he muttered, under his breath.
How he had tried
to save the cities-!
but good men are hard to find;
no matter how he begged
that was God's condition
to spare the town from fire and perdition.

So they fled-
never looking 'round
despite the soughing sound
that left the town a city of the dead,
and never ceased, but travelled day and night
until the earliest streak of golden light
when, stopped to rest beneath a tamarind tree,
where once were four, he counted only three

Love Poem Without Commas

like twin ghazal of origin co-eval
each a brandish bound and confessional
falling satellite-like through the seven rings
of very little I quit balking to recall
the futility of anything's everything:
the this-new-old-world-agricultural
all-clinging mache of meaning
dependable and workable

Until
crossing the rainbow of you
with your secret smile
space lit all its candles, colorful
as old crystal, beginning an indefinite while.

Now I'm a cat up the tree of your good will
firemen circle the base: breath-taking some;
soon they'll try to fetch me—what a pill!
Over there's a truck, red as the sun—
I watch all through my diamond slits-
Axes axe. Pennants flap. Ladders lean
reaching to a heartthrob big as the Ritz
even I cannot deny.

Heart you're a billibong
ringed by a fetid strand
wider than long
on whose reeking rand
chuck themselves up more-or-less prehistoric fish
that gasp themselves out-melt into the sand,
fuming a stinking nimbus
that rising, wick-like covers all the land.

Show Tune #5

When you walked into the room
My heart hit the ceiling
You were the one for me
There was no concealing
Something in your smile I found
So endlessly appealing
You restore my heart to
Its era of Good Feeling.

There was a time . . .

Your pumps were so pretty
In all the sparkling city
Maybe the prettiest-
Slick the way they fit you
And your dress of whitest eyelet
That swung about your knees
Couldn't hide, couldn't hide
What was inside

There was a time . . .

You didn't tipple, dear-
just a little bubbly
Never was anyone so clever!
Never was anything so lovely!
Like a melody by Stephen Foster
Endlessly, endlessly
You go through my head
Through my head.

There was a time . . .

All at once we're dancing.
A thousand little lamps glister
As the basses lead our feet
Around and the cymbals sigh and whisper
On the ground or in the air
Love never lets you down
Heads you win, tails I lose
Never sounded better!

There was a time, oh,
When high brows was low brows
People little know now
The way it was, then
But we do, dear, and now
We're here to rock and roll again!
Never touch, that's for lovers-
Save it for later. And how!

Kosko Cat

1,3,2,4,1,3,2,4,1,

3...2....4.....

stop, sit, scratch, slip
under the rail and disappear.

Swans

Unruffled, they sailed the seas
wings set back on racks of air
blown stiffly by the breeze
quasi-mechanically
showing the world no care;
or like a canon with twin themes
tread the crisp air
softly, like brothers
heeling shore to shore.

Now back and forth, they swing
placid in my mind
drawing dreams on dream
by ribbons and tangled tethers in their bills—
The only labor due them
because they never sing
for that would mean their death's come, so they go
mutely drifting, studying their faces in the quick
dipping their heads below

in liquid jade
I recall one sorry soul
call them, by riverside,
vessels of treachery
that haul unwary children down
to walk the murky bottom, and so drown
like Gulliver, bound
in sodden reed to helpless fixity-
yet, of treachery they seemed to me

Guiltless-they
never flustered me
but like a player in a play
I tossed them crusts of bread
and tufts of candy cotton, pink and green
onto the solvent scene
all the which they gratefully received
thanked me dumbly and retrieved
with gracious nods and blue shakes of the head.

All so very, very
supernumerary
yet could one
name the names of all:
a dozen dozen
distinguishable
doughtily paddling in tandem
brother by brother, cousin by cousin
or alone by preference at random,

There was Water-Wing and Water-Weary
Clamor and Flotsome and Fade,
the lovely, sinuous O'Leary;
Then dumb Mute and peerless Wade
came a-begging.
led by Sulphur-Cheek and Feather-Legging
Bottom and Crester
and the dark Trumpeter
studying themselves in the water's mirror.

And many, many more
along an endless shore
their light-militia up the flood extended
fierce and sotto-sounding
further than the eye could see
irked as if they had to pay
mortgages, with fees compounding
on which their days depended
but, actually, they didn't, needing nay.

Then came a dawn
so odd, I can't forget:
down in a desultory way
fell the snows of morn, that winter's day.
All turned, acceding to one will
over the water sped and faster till
each vanished, drawn
into the low-set clouds like jet succeeding jet
clutching his fellow's tail in his own bill.

I can only wonder where
Water-Wing and Weary
Clamor, Flotsome, Fade
lovely sinuous O'Leary
Sulphur-Cheek and Feather-Legging were;
and Feather-Bed Feather-Head and Fade
I would greet them there-
where Mute is, Trumpeter and Wade-
whose eye was pink and twinkled like the Morning Star.

Anniversary

The kitchen calendar, impaled by a nail in the wall,
thumbed by the breeze over the still-damp floor,
its edges stamped with dates
under Fantin La Tour plates,
is the wind's rolodex;
the blue-filled edges of each gridded square,
like window boxes after April snow,
say it's been a week beyond a year
since your long, inelegant demise, mother, dear.

Again, I see you snatched from the doldrums of Providence
where the streets had names like Main, Mt Pleasant and Charles,
transported from the football fields of Providence,
so quiet, one could say rosaries,
despair, a ticking clock,
the loveliest orphan on the block,
trusting only in what's plain: God's choosey grace,
that awesome provost, his Holy Ghost
and your own sweet face.

Again, I hear you shouting awake
the sleepers sleeping
keeping house for your spouse
a vile privilege, no mistake,
disappointment the sort of natural glue:
it wasn't designed to be.
your pools of grace
dwindled sadly, as time wore on, and only God
once so friendly, to blame.

I hear the tales that told us who we were:
the corn-copping deer that bounded from the barn at dawn;
the wolves that crept down and howled in the foothills;
The squaw that came calling, and, unlike Whitman's stayed;
the supervised rite of the college dance
where future soul-mates met by chance.
You clapped each year when I unwrapped
the sackbut-playing shepherd in yellow hose—
a gift from Grace.

Understanding comes in waves and if waves
delay or come too breathlessly
out of the future or the past,
it doesn't matter, everything adding up and cancelling out.
From the golden fields of youth and Need
to the inevitable let-down of time
things happen differently
than we expect them to—
Purity is all.

Mother, beauty
worthy to be sculpted by Pisano,
you thought you had a hotline to God;
which, in fact, you did,
via cables of infinite trust.
Some guess righteousness a proof against misfortune—
It isn't always. Others say you get what you deserve.

Desert? Awful
to say what anyone deserves:
desert the moity of a harsher ethic
incomprehensible to the catholic mind.
In the end, who doesn't deserve grace?
Faust, stepped from glibness, held his tongue.
Nobody knows *nothing*—you're a fool if you say you do.
There's payment for each transgression—
but, Mother, you didn't deserve this.

Remembering Christmas

A small dark plane is parked outside the complex.
The glistening snow screens a span of wings.
On the fuselage—Fox News or something.
The crew flaps their arms against the cold.

The ground is littered with boxes and cables.
Men decide the best place to pitch the cameras.
Candles burn tall at a table decked with holly.
It has stopped snowing. All is merry and bright.

There on the terrace sits Mrs. Claus, —herself
Mittened, swaddled in a fur-lined parka
The slightly-embarrassed focus of so much attention,
But growing steadily more and more at home.

She is talking to an interviewer—no, a team of them
Having decided (why not?) in favor of mikes
Of which six whistle-crackle in an arc before her
Beside a platter of still-warm Christmas cookies

Into the microphone she says, '*Yes*, I pack the gifts.'
Wrapping each in plasticene or muslin.
Yes, she packs the Mister's lunch and dinner.
It's a long way around the world, isn't it, now,

Including the beers-not too many nor too few
To keep the chill off and make the traveling light
And steel him for that intercontinental flight
Dark and tumultuous, over the Bering Strait.

Yes, she likes the deer, laying in for each
An extra measure of hay before they fly
Wetly kissing each one's nose,
Wishing the great creatures godspeed.

They lower their heads, snort, and paw the
Ground, alert to her attention
Then she waves, draws her coat about her
As the caravan begins to race, the whip crack,

With an 'onward, fellows', over the frozen turf,
Faster and faster, like a 747,
Until suddenly airborn, gone and flying past the moon,
Leaving her in the shadowy stillness.

'No', she never wanted to fly them . . .
Even as many times as she's seen it done
It's the Mister's schtick—who needs it-
The wild descent, the wind, the ashes

In the tertiary bronchioles—forget it. Besides,
It's been years since she's been down a chimney.
Besides, expectation being the essence of the season,
They're expecting him.

The light on the frozen snow is astral.
Outshining the paltry sheen from the kliegs
It reminds her of something that happened long ago
She can't say just what it was, now, though.

The interview is over—the crew is packing up.
The plane is loaded, all hands aboard:
Goodbye, goodbye. The co-pilot winks and signals.
Over the tundra taxies the little plane,

Faster and faster, then off! It turns, bisects the piñata-moon,
Spilling a rain of musical toys:
Tom-tom, tin whistle, kazoo—on the snow-clad peaks
Under Polaris, twinkling straight above.

Onto the glacier, onto the ghostly slopes,
Into the vallies between crags, the fir-lined foothills
Skidding down icey jags, alongside rivers
Of black, moon-stuck billows,

Coming to rest at her feet. She picks one up, toots
Experimentally, watches the plane till the wing lights fade
Or longer and turns—
Time to go in. 'Tomorrow, Clause will be home'.